联合国

How We Organize Ourselves | Non-Fiction Series

Copyright © 2022 by Level Learning, INC. and Washington Yu Ying PCS™
Original and Edited Text Copyright © 2022 by Washington Yu Ying PCS™

All rights reserved. No part of this book in whole or part may be reproduced without written permission from the publisher.

Published by Level Learning, INC.

Content Contributors:
Washington Yu Ying PCS™ - Jianhua (Allen) Zhong, Pearl Zao He You
Level Learning - Jingyao Qi

Illustrations by: Josh Taira

Leveling classification based on Level Learning standard.
For full description, visit www.levellearning.com

ISBN 978-1-64040-112-9
Simplified Chinese Edition

About Level Learning:
Level Learning provides a literacy focused curriculum specifically designed for K-12 Chinese as a Second Language classrooms. Our program offers 20 levels of specific and detailed objectives, leveled texts and passages, mastery-based online assessment, and analytics to enable data-driven instruction. Level Learning reading curriculum for both literature and informational text emphasize grammar and comprehension skills to help teachers develop confident and independent Chinese language readers. The non-fiction series of books are specifically designed to support our informational text course based on multiple national standards. To learn more about our entire offering, visit www.levellearning.com.

About Washington Yu Ying PCS™:
Washington Yu Ying PCS is a Mandarin English dual language immersion International Baccalaureate (IB) World school. Yu Ying's mission is to inspire and prepare young people to create a better world by challenging them to reach their full potential in a nurturing Chinese/English educational environment. Yu Ying's comprehensive IB, dual immersion curriculum equips students with global competencies for success in the real world. As a leader in immersion education, Yu Ying is determined to advance Chinese language programs and global citizenry education by helping other schools create and strengthen their Chinese programs. For more information, email: products@washingtonyuying.org

联合国成立于1945年，到2017年，联合国一共有193个成员国。

CHINA
中国

SECURITY COUNCIL
联合国安理会

ENGLAND
英国

USA
美国

FRANCE
法国

RUSSIA
俄罗斯

联合国有五个最重要的成员国,这五个成员国是美国、英国、法国、中国和俄罗斯。

联合国的成立是为了维护世界和平,联合国的成立是为了帮助有需要的人。

联合国每年开一次联合国大会,大家一起讨论世界上发生的重要的事情。比如说,维护世界和平,帮助妇女和儿童等等。

有了联合国,世界更和平了,有了联合国,很多需要帮助的人得到了帮助。

联合国总部在美国纽约，你有时间的话，去联合国总部看看吧。

Glossary

	Pinyin	English Definition
联合国	lián hé guó	United Nations
成立	chéng lì	to establish
成员国	chéng yuán guó	member nation
重要	zhòng yào	important
维护	wéi hù	to defend, to protect
和平	hé píng	peace
帮助	bāng zhù	to help
需要	xū yào	need
开	kāi	to hold
会	huì	general assembly, meeting
讨论	tǎo lùn	to discuss
事情	shì qing	issues
妇女	fù nǚ	women

	Pinyin	English Definition
儿童	ér tóng	children
更	gèng	even more
总部	zǒng bù	headquarter
纽约	niǔ yuē	New York

www.ingramcontent.com/pod-product-compliance
Lightning Source LLC
Chambersburg PA
CBHW041227070526
44584CB00001B/125